FLOURY FINGERS

GW00669888

FLOURY FINGERS

by

CECILIA H. HINDE

illustrated by

JEAN HINDE

Floury Fingers
Buttery Nose.
That's the way
The Cooking Goes

FABER AND FABER LIMITED

London

First published in 1962
by Faber and Faber Limited
*24 Russell Square London W.C.*1
First published in this edition 1969
Reprinted 1970
Printed in Great Britain by
Latimer Trend & Co Ltd Whitstable
All rights reserved
SBN (*paper bound*) 571 09075 3
SBN (*hard bound*) 571 04522 7

© *Cecilia H. Hinde*
1962

CONDITIONS OF SALE

This book is sold subject to the condition that it shall not, by way of trade or otherwise, be lent, re-sold, hired out or otherwise circulated without the publisher's prior consent in any form of binding or cover other than that in which it is published and without a similar condition including this condition being imposed on the subsequent purchaser

CONTENTS

6 *CONTENTS*

INTRODUCTION

'FLOURY FINGERS'

This is a book for very young children to use. The actions are given step by step, with each stage clearly illustrated.

The ingredients are measured by cups and spoons. I realize that this does not make for absolute accuracy, but accuracy is not my chief concern, although, of course, it is important.

In this book, I have tried to give the child recipes of things that she can make on her own, using implements with which she is familiar. I have put them as simply as possible, so that she can read them for herself. To facilitate this, where the actions are repeated from recipe to recipe, I have tried to use the same wording in each case.

As this is a book for small children, I have used only those recipes which require the minimum of contact with the hot stove. Nor are there recipes which require boiling or frying. I have left out all mixtures which have to be creamed or well beaten, as this is probably beyond their strength.

There are one or two cooking terms, such as 'knead', 'sprinkle', which I have had to use and which will need to be demonstrated.

This book can be used in the home or at school. The recipes are simple and the ingredients small, so that several children can cook at the same time. In most cases the cooking time is short. This means that the oven, at home or at school, needs to be used for the minimum amount of time only.

In measuring, 'big spoons' are tablespoons and 'small spoons' are teaspoons. Where fats are used it will facilitate measuring if they are warmed slightly.

C. H. H.

TO COOKS WITH 'FLOURY FINGERS'

This is your book.
I have made it
as easy as I can for you.
But there are one or two things
that are rather hard to do,
like 'knead' and 'sprinkle'.
Mummy will show you what to do.
It is rather hard
to beat up an egg with a fork.
Mummy will show you
how to do this as well.
Or she may let you
use her egg beater.
If she does,
use it very carefully.

The sweets are rather special.
None of them are cooked
so eat them up soon
or they will get very hard.

One last thing.
When you have finished cooking,
wash up all your things
and dry them
and put them away.
Clean your table and the floor

if you have spilt anything.
Do not leave anything
for Mummy to do.

I hope you like this book
and have lots of fun with it.

SMALL CHERRY CAKES

Ask Mummy to put the oven on at
Electric 450 or Gas Regulo 8

You Will Want

FLOUR Self Raising		**SMALL BASIN**	
SALT		**CUP** For measuring	
MARGARINE		**SIEVE**	
CASTER SUGAR		**WOODEN SPOON** For mixing	
CHERRIES Glacé		**FORK**	
EGG		**KNIFE**	
MILK In a cup		**2 BIG SPOONS**	
ESSENCE Vanilla		**PAPER CASES** or small cake tins	
BIG BASIN		**BAKING SHEET**	

Now put on your overall
and wash your hands.

Take the big basin and the sieve.
Put the sieve over the basin.
Now into the sieve put

FLOUR . . . . One (1) cup
SALT . . . . One (1) pinch
Shake your sieve until all the flour
and salt have fallen into the basin.
Take off the sieve.

Put into the basin

MARGARINE . . . . . Two (2) big spoons,
. . . . rounded

Now rub together
the flour and the fat.
Do it with your finger-tips
until there are no more lumps of fat
left in the flour.
Then wash your hands.

Count out

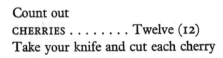

CHERRIES . . . . Twelve (12)
Take your knife and cut each cherry

into four (4) pieces.
Drop them into the flour.
Next put into the basin
SUGAR .... Three (3) big spoons.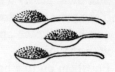
Take your wooden spoon
and mix them all together.
When it is mixed
make a hole in the middle
ready for the egg.
Now take the small basin and the
EGG.
Break the egg into the small basin
and with the fork
beat up the egg.
Then from the cup take
MILK .... Two (2) big spoons.
Put it into the egg.
Add a few drops of
VANILLA ESSENCE.
Ask Mummy to do this.
Stir them all together.
Pour into the hole in the big basin

and with your wooden spoon
mix them gently together.
Take your cake cases
and half fill each one
with the mixture.
Put them on to a baking sheet.
Ask Mummy to put them into the oven.
Leave them there for about
15 MINUTES.
Tell Mummy
when it is time to take them out.
When they are cool
you can ice some of them
and decorate with cherries,
silver balls, nuts or angelica.

SMALL FRUIT CAKES

*Ask Mummy to put the oven on at
Electric 450 or Gas Regulo 8*

YOU WILL WANT

FLOUR
Self Raising

SALT

MARGARINE

CASTER SUGAR

EGG

MILK
In a cup

CURRANTS

SULTANAS

CHOPPED PEEL
If you like it

BIG BASIN

SMALL BASIN

CUP
For measuring

SIEVE

WOODEN SPOON
For mixing

FORK

2 BIG SPOONS

SMALL CAKE TINS
Or paper cases

BAKING SHEET

Now put on your overall
and wash your hands.

Take the big basin and the sieve.
Put the sieve over the basin.
Now into the sieve put
FLOUR . . . . .One (1) cup.
SALT. . . . . .One (1) pinch.
Shake the sieve until all the flour
and salt have fallen into the basin.
Take off the sieve.
Put into the basin
MARGARINE . . . . .Two (2) big spoons,
. . . . .rounded.
Now rub together
the flour and the fat.
Do it with your finger tips
until there are no more lumps of fat
left in the flour.
Then wash your hands.
Next put into the basin
SUGAR . . . . .Three (3) big spoons.

CURRANTS.......One (1) big spoon.

SULTANAS.......One (1) big spoon.

If you want it fruity,

put in a little more.

PEEL...........One (1) small spoon.

Mix together with your finger-tips.

When it is mixed

make a hole in the middle

ready for the egg.

Now take the small basin and the

EGG.

Break the egg into the small basin

and with the fork

beat up the egg.

Then from the cup take

MILK ....Two (2) big spoons.

Put it into the egg

and stir them together.

Pour it into the hole in the big basin

and with your wooden spoon

mix them gently together.

Take your small cake cases
and half fill each one
with the mixture.
Put them on to a baking sheet.
Ask Mummy to put them into the oven.
Leave them there for about
15 MINUTES.
Tell Mummy
when it is time to take them out.
When they are cool you can ice them
and decorate with nuts
and angelica.

ROCK CAKES

Ask Mummy to put the oven on at
Electric 450 or Gas Regulo 8

You Will Want

FLOUR
Self raising

CUP
For measuring

SALT

SMALL BASIN

MARGARINE

SIEVE

CASTER SUGAR

FORK

CURRANTS

SMALL SPOON

EGG

2 BIG SPOONS
For measuring

MILK
In a cup

WOODEN SPOON
For mixing

CHOPPED PEEL
If you like it

BIG BASIN

BAKING SHEET
Rub it with a bit of
margarine paper to
make it greasy

Put on your overall
and wash your hands.

Take the big basin and the sieve.
Put the sieve over the basin.
Now into the sieve put

FLOUR . . . . One (1) cup.
SALT . . . . One (1) pinch.
Shake the sieve
until all the flour and salt
have fallen into the basin.
Take off the sieve.
Next, put into the basin
MARGARINE . . . . . Two (2) big spoons,
. . . . rounded.
Now rub together the flour and fat.
Do it with your finger-tips
until there are no more lumps of fat
left in the flour.
Then wash your hands.

Next put into the basin

SUGAR .... Three (3) big spoons.

CURRANTS....... Four (4) big spoons.

CHOPPED PEEL...One (1) small spoon.

Take your wooden spoon
and mix them all together.
Now make a hole in the middle
ready for the egg and milk.
Take the small basin and the
EGG.
Break the egg into the small basin
and with the fork
beat up the egg.
Then take out

EGG ....One (1) big spoon.

Pour it into the hole in the big basin.
Then from the cup take

MILK ....Two (2) small spoons,

and put into the big basin too.
Stir together with the wooden spoon.
If it is too dry, put in more egg.
Do not make it too wet.

Sprinkle a little flour
on to your baking sheet.
Fill your small spoon
with the mixture
and with your fork
scrape it off in lumps
on to your baking sheet.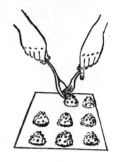
Leave a space between each one.
Ask Mummy
to put them into the oven.
Leave them there for about
15 MINUTES.
Tell Mummy
when it is time
to take them out.

COCONUT BUNS

Ask Mummy to put the oven on at
Electric 450 or Gas Regulo 8

You Will Want

FLOUR Self Raising		CUP For measuring	
SALT		SIEVE	
MARGARINE		FORK	
CASTER SUGAR		2 BIG SPOONS For measuring	
COCONUT		SMALL SPOON For measuring	
EGG			
MILK In a cup		WOODEN SPOON For mixing	
BIG BASIN		BAKING SHEET Rub it with a bit of margarine paper to make it greasy	
SMALL BASIN			

Put on your overall
and wash your hands.

Take the big basin and the sieve.
Put the sieve over the basin.
Now into the sieve put

FLOUR . . . . One (1) cup.
SALT . . . . One (1) pinch.
Shake your sieve
until all the flour and salt
have fallen into the basin.
Take off the sieve.
Next, put into the basin
MARGARINE . . . . . . Two (2) big spoons,
. . . . rounded.

Now rub together the flour and fat.
Do it with your finger-tips
until there are no more lumps of fat
left in the flour.
Then wash your hands.

Next put into the basin

SUGAR . . . . Three (3) big spoons.

COCONUT . . . . Six (6) small spoons,

. . . . heaped.

Take your wooden spoon
and mix them all together.
Now make a hole in the middle
ready for the egg and milk.
Take the small basin and the

EGG.

Break the egg into the small basin
and with the fork
beat up the egg.
Then take out

EGG . . . . One (1) big spoon.

Pour it into the hole in the big basin.
Then from the cup take

MILK . . . . Three (3) small spoons.

and put into the big basin too.
Stir together with the wooden spoon.
If it is too dry, put in more egg.
Do not make it too wet.

Sprinkle a little flour
on to your baking sheet.
Fill your small spoon
with the mixture
and with your fork
scrape it off in lumps
on to your baking sheet.
Leave a space between each one.
Ask Mummy
to put them into the oven.
Leave them there for about
15 MINUTES.
Tell Mummy
when it is time
to take them out.
When they are cool,
decorate each coconut bun
with a piece of cherry.

JAM BUNS

Ask Mummy to put the oven on at
Electric 450 or Gas Regulo 8

You Will Want

FLOUR Self Raising		SIEVE	
		PASTRY BRUSH	
SALT			
MARGARINE		2 BIG SPOONS For measuring	
CASTER SUGAR		WOODEN SPOON For mixing	
MILK In a cup		KNIFE	
JAM		BAKING SHEET Rub it with a bit of margarine paper to make it greasy	
BIG BASIN			

Put on your overall
and wash your hands.

Take the big basin and the sieve.
Put the sieve over the basin.
Now into the sieve put
FLOUR . . . . One (1) cup.
SALT. . . . . One (1) pinch.
Shake the sieve
until all the flour and salt
have fallen into the basin.
Take off the sieve.
Next, put into the basin
MARGARINE. . . . . . Two (2) big spoons,
. . . . rounded.
Now rub together the flour and fat.
Do it with your finger-tips
until there are no more lumps of fat
left in the flour.
Then wash your hands.
Next put in
SUGAR . . . . Two (2) big spoons.
Take your wooden spoon
and mix it together.
Pour in
MILK . . . . Two (2) big spoons,
and stir it in.

If it is too dry, put in more milk.
Do not make it sticky.
Sprinkle a little flour
on to the table.
Tip the mixture out of the basin.
Knead it with your hands
until it is smooth.
Now take your knife
and cut it up into about
Nine (9) pieces.
Take each piece
and roll it into a ball.
Put them on to the baking sheet.
Leave a space between each one.
Then with your finger
poke a hole in the top of each bun
and put in some JAM.
Dip your pastry brush
into the milk
and paint over the top
of each bun.
Now ask Mummy
to put them into the oven.
Leave them there for about
10–12 MINUTES.
Tell Mummy
when it is time to take them out.

~~~~~~

CHOCOLATE CRISPIES

Ask Mummy to put the oven on at
Electric 350 or Gas Regulo 4

Now ask her to please make you
HALF A CUP OF MELTED BUTTER

You Will Want As Well

PLAIN FLOUR		BIG BASIN	
CASTER SUGAR		BLUNT KNIFE For mixing	
CORNFLAKES		SMALL SPOON	
SALT		BIG SPOON	
TIN OF DRINKING CHOCOLATE		CUP For measuring	
		BAKING SHEET	

Wash your hands. Overall on.

Take the big basin and into it put
CORNFLAKES.....One (1) cup.
SALT............One (1) pinch.
SUGAR ....Three (3) big spoons.
PLAIN FLOUR ....Two (2) big spoons,
...............rounded.
DRINKING
CHOCOLATE......Three (3) big spoons.
Mix them all together
with your blunt knife.
Now pour in
MELTED BUTTER. Half a cup.
Do this very carefully.
Mix them all together
with your blunt knife.

With your small spoon
drop the mixture
on to the baking sheet
in little heaps.
Leave a space
between each.
Ask Mummy
to put them into the oven.
Leave them there for about
15 MINUTES.
When they come out of the oven
do not touch them
until they are cool
or they will break into pieces.
Put them into an air-tight tin
to keep them crisp.

DATE FINGERS

Ask Mummy to put the oven on at
Electric 350 or Gas Regulo 4

You Will Want

SWEETENED CONDENSED MILK		BIG BASIN	
PLAIN FLOUR		BLUNT KNIFE For mixing	
BAKING POWDER		KNIFE	
SALT		BIG SPOON For measuring	
CHOPPED DATES			
BIG SPOON OF CHOPPED NUTS		SWISS ROLL TIN Rub with a piece of buttery paper	

~~~~~~

Wash your hands. Overall on.

Take the big basin and into it put
SWEETENED
CONDENSED MILK Three (3) big spoons.
FLOUR . . . . Two (2) big spoons,
. . . . .rounded.

BAKING POWDER .One (1) pinch.
SALT . . . . .One (1) pinch.
CHOPPED DATES. . Two (2) big spoons.
CHOPPED NUTS. . .One (1) big spoon.
Mix them all together
with your blunt knife.
Tip the mixture
into the tin.
Spread it with your knife.
Ask Mummy
to put it into the oven.
Leave it there for about
25 MINUTES.
When it comes out
ask Mummy
to please cut it up into fingers.

HONEY CRUNCH

Ask Mummy to put the oven on at
Electric 350 or Gas Regulo 4

You Will Want

BUTTER		CUP For measuring	
HONEY		2 BIG SPOONS	
CASTER SUGAR			
		SMALL SPOON	
PUFFED WHEAT		BLUNT KNIFE For mixing	
		TART TINS	
BIG BASIN For mixing			

Grease these with a
bit of buttery paper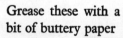

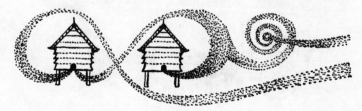

Wash your hands. Overall on.

Take the big basin
and into it put

CASTER SUGAR . . . Three (3) big spoons.
HONEY . . . . Two (2) big spoons.
BUTTER . . . . One (1) big spoon,
. . . . rounded.

Ask Mummy
to please put the basin
into the oven.

Leave it there for about 5 MINUTES,
until everything has melted
and please take it out again.
When Mummy says
that the basin is cool enough,
put in

PUFFED WHEAT . . . Three (3) cups.
Stir everything together
with your blunt knife.

Now take your small spoon.
Fill it with the mixture
and drop it in lumps
into the tart tins.
Ask Mummy
to put them into the oven.
Leave them there
for about 8–10 MINUTES.
When they come out of the oven
do not touch them
until they are cool
or they will break into pieces.
If they stick in the tart tins,
ask Mummy to warm them gently
and lift them out.
Put them into an air-tight tin
to keep them crisp.

PLAIN SCONES

*Ask Mummy to put the oven on at
Electric 475 or Gas Regulo 9*

You Will Want

FLOUR
Self Raising

SALT

MARGARINE

MILK
In a cup

BIG BASIN

ROLLING-PIN

CUTTER

BLUNT KNIFE

PASTRY BRUSH

SIEVE

SMALL SPOON
For measuring

BIG SPOON
For measuring

CUP
For measuring

BAKING SHEET
Rub it with a bit of
margarine paper to
make it greasy

See that your hands are clean
and your overall on.

Take the big basin and the sieve
Put the sieve over the basin.
Now put into it

FLOUR .... One (1) cup, heaped.
SALT .... One (1) pinch.

Shake the sieve
until all the flour and salt
have fallen into the basin.
Take off the sieve.
Put into the basin

MARGARINE ...... Two (2) small spoons
.... rounded.

Now rub together the flour and fat.
Do it with your finger-tips
until there are no more lumps of fat
left in the flour.
Then wash your hands.
Pour in the

MILK .... Four (4) big spoons.

Stir quickly with your blunt knife.
You have to hurry now
or your scones will be spoilt.
Sprinkle flour on to the table.
Tip out the mixture
and pat it to make it round.
Take your rolling-pin.
Sprinkle it with flour
and roll out the mixture until it is
half ($\frac{1}{2}$) an inch thick.
Take your cutter,
dip it into the flour,
cut out round scones
and place them on the baking sheet.
Gather up the pieces,
quickly make them into a round
and cut out more scones,
until all the bits are used up.
Dip your pastry brush into the milk
and paint the tops of the scones.
This will make them shiny brown
when they are cooked.

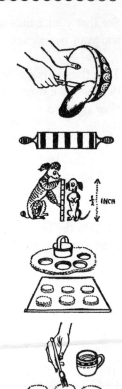

Do all these things quickly.
Now ask Mummy
to put them into the oven.
Leave them there until they are brown,
about 8–10 MINUTES.
Tell Mummy
when it is time to take them out.
When they are cooled a little
split them in half
and butter them.
If you want them sweet
put jam on to each half scone.
If you like tomatoes instead,
put a slice
on to each piece of scone.

SWEET SCONES

*Ask Mummy to put the oven on at
Electric 475 or Gas Regulo 9*

You Will Want

FLOUR
Self Raising

SALT

MARGARINE

MILK
In a cup

CASTER SUGAR

BIG BASIN

ROLLING-PIN

CUTTER

PASTRY BRUSH

SIEVE

BIG SPOON
For measuring

SMALL SPOON
For measuring

CUP
For measuring

BLUNT KNIFE

BAKING SHEET
Rub it with a bit of
margarine paper to
make it greasy

See that your hands are clean
and your overall on.

Take the big basin and the sieve.
Put the sieve over the basin.
Now put into it

FLOUR ....One (1) cup, heaped.
SALT............One (1) pinch.
Shake the sieve
until all the flour and salt
have fallen into the basin.
Take off the sieve.
Put into the basin

MARGARINE......Two (2) small spoons,
...............rounded.
Now rub together the flour and fat.
Do it with your finger-tips
until there are no more lumps of fat
left in the flour.
Then wash your hands.

Put in
CASTER SUGAR ...One (1) big spoon,
and stir it in.
Pour in the

MILK ....Four (4) big spoons.
Stir quickly with your blunt knife.
You have to hurry now
or your scones will be spoilt.
Sprinkle flour on to the table.

Tip out the mixture
and pat it to make it round.
Take your rolling-pin.
Sprinkle it with flour
and roll out the mixture until it is
Half ($\frac{1}{2}$) an inch thick.

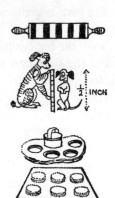

Take your cutter,
dip it into the flour,
cut out round scones
and place them on the baking sheet.

Gather up the pieces,
quickly make them into a round
and cut out more scones
until all the bits are used up.
Dip your pastry brush into the milk
and paint the tops of the scones.
This will make them shiny brown
when they are cooked.

Do all these things quickly.
Now ask Mummy
to put them into the oven.
Leave them there until they are brown,
about 8–10 MINUTES.
Tell Mummy
when it is time to take them out.

When they are cooled a little,
split them in half
and butter them.

~~~~~~

FRUIT SCONES

Ask Mummy to put the oven on at
Electric 475 or Gas Regulo 9

You Will Want

FLOUR Self Raising	**CUTTER**
SALT	**BLUNT KNIFE**
MARGARINE	**PASTRY BRUSH**
	SIEVE
MILK In a cup	**2 SMALL SPOONS** For measuring
CASTER SUGAR	**BIG SPOON** For measuring
SULTANAS	
BIG BASIN	**CUP** For measuring
ROLLING-PIN	**BAKING SHEET** Rub it with a bit of margarine paper to make it greasy

See that your hands are clean
and your overall on.

Take the big basin and the sieve.
Put the sieve over the basin.
Now put into it

FLOUR . . . . One (1) cup, heaped
SALT. . . . . One (1) pinch.
Shake the sieve
until all the flour and salt
have fallen into the basin.
Take off the sieve.
Put into the basin

MARGARINE. . . . . . Two (2) small spoons
. . . . rounded.
Now rub together the flour and fat.
Do it with your finger-tips
until there are no more lumps of fat
left in the flour.

Then wash your hands.
Put in
CASTER SUGAR . . . Three (3) small spoons.

SULTANAS . . . . One (1) big spoon.
Mix them in with your finger-tips.
Pour in the
MILK . . . . Four (4) big spoons.
Stir quickly with your blunt knife.
Now you will have to hurry
or your scones will be spoilt.
Sprinkle flour on the table.
Tip out the mixture
and pat it to make it round.
Take your rolling-pin.
Sprinkle it with flour
and roll out the mixture until it is
half (½) an inch thick.
Take your cutter,
dip it into the flour,
cut out round scones
and place them on the baking sheet.
Gather up the pieces,
quickly make them into a round
and cut out more scones
until all the bits are used up.

Dip your pastry brush into the milk
and paint the tops of the scones.
This will make them shiny brown
when they are cooked.
Do all these things quickly.
Now ask Mummy
to put them into the oven.
Leave them there until they are brown,
about 8–10 MINUTES.
Tell Mummy
when it is time to take them out.
When they are cooled a little,
split them in half
and butter them.

TEA-PARTY SCONES

Ask Mummy to put the oven on at
Electric 475 or Gas Regulo 9

You Will Want

FLOUR Self Raising	**SMALL BASIN**
	ROLLING-PIN
SALT	**CUTTER**
MARGARINE	**BLUNT KNIFE**
MILK In a cup	**FORK**
CASTER SUGAR	**PASTRY BRUSH**
	SIEVE
SULTANAS	
RAISINS *or* **CURRANTS**	**2 SMALL SPOONS** For measuring
EGG	**CUP**
	BAKING SHEET Rub it with a bit of margarine paper to make it greasy
BIG BASIN	

See that your hands are clean
and your overall on.

Take the big basin and the sieve.
Put the sieve over the basin.
Now put into it

FLOUR . . . . One (1) cup, heaped.
SALT. . . . . One (1) pinch.
Shake the sieve
until all the flour and salt
have fallen into the basin.
Take off the sieve.
Put into the basin
MARGARINE. . . . . . Two (2) small spoons,
. . . . rounded.
Now rub together the flour and fat.
Do it with your finger-tips
until there are no more lumps of fat
left in the flour.
Then wash your hands.
Put in
CASTER SUGAR . . . Four (4) small spoons.
SULTANAS . . . . Two (2) small spoons.

RAISINS or
CURRANTS........Two (2) small spoons.
Mix them in with your finger-tips.
Now take the small basin and the
EGG.
Break the egg into the small basin
and with the fork
beat up the egg.
Then from the cup take
MILK ....Two (2) big spoons.
Put it into the egg
and stir them together.
Pour into the big basin.
Stir quickly with your blunt knife.
Now you have to hurry
or your scones will be spoilt.
Sprinkle flour on to the table.
Tip out the mixture
and pat it to make it round.
Take your rolling-pin.
Sprinkle it with flour
and roll out the mixture until it is
half (½) an inch thick.

Take your cutter,
dip it into the flour,
cut out round scones
and place them on the baking sheet.
Gather up the pieces,
quickly make them into a round
and cut out more scones
until all the bits are used up.
Dip your pastry brush into the milk
and paint the tops of the scones.
This will make them shiny brown
when they are cooked.
Do all these things quickly.
Now ask Mummy
to put them into the oven.
Leave them there until they are brown,
about 8–10 MINUTES.
Tell Mummy
when it is time to take them out.
When they are cooled a little
split them in half
and butter them.

DATE SCONES

Ask Mummy to put the oven on at
Electric 475 or Gas Regulo 9

You Will Want

FLOUR Self Raising		BLUNT KNIFE	
SALT		PASTRY BRUSH	
MARGARINE		SIEVE	
MILK In a cup		2 SMALL SPOONS For measuring	
CASTER SUGAR	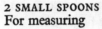	BIG SPOON For measuring	
CHOPPED DATES		CUP For measuring	
BIG BASIN			
ROLLING-PIN		BAKING SHEET Rub it with a bit of margarine paper to make it greasy	
CUTTER			

See that your hands are clean
and your overall on.

Take the big basin and the sieve.
Put the sieve over the basin.
Now put into it
FLOUR .... One (1) cup, heaped.
SALT............ One (1) pinch.
Shake the sieve
until all the flour and salt
have fallen into the basin.
Take off the sieve.
Put into the basin

MARGARINE...... Two (2) small spoons
.... rounded.
Now rub together the flour and fat.
Do it with your finger-tips
until there are no more lumps of fat
left in the flour.
Then wash your hands.
Put in

CASTER SUGAR ... Three (3) small spoons.

CHOPPED DATES.. Two (2) big spoons.
Mix them in with your finger-tips.
Pour in the

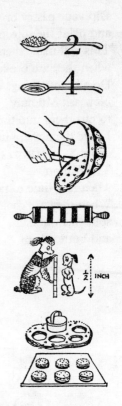

MILK .... Four (4) big spoons.
Stir quickly with your blunt knife.
Now you will have to hurry
or your scones will be spoilt.
Sprinkle flour on to the table.
Tip out the mixture
and pat it to make it round.
Take your rolling-pin.
Sprinkle it with flour
and roll out the mixture until it is
half (½) an inch thick.
Take your cutter,
dip it in the flour,
cut out round scones
and place them on the baking sheet.
Gather up the pieces,
quickly make them into a round
and cut out more scones
until all the bits are used up.

Dip your pastry brush into the milk
and paint the tops of the scones.
This will make them shiny brown
when they are cooked.
Do all these things quickly.
Now ask Mummy
to put them into the oven.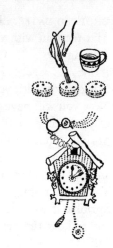
Leave them there until they are brown,
about 8–10 MINUTES.
Tell Mummy
when it is time to take them out.
When they are cooled a little,
split them in half
and butter them.

CHEESE SCONES

Ask Mummy to put the oven on at
Electric 475 or Gas Regulo 9

You Will Want

FLOUR Self Raising		**BLUNT KNIFE**	
SALT		**PASTRY BRUSH**	
MARGARINE		**SIEVE**	
MILK In a cup		**SMALL SPOON** For measuring	
GRATED CHEESE		**BIG SPOON** For measuring	
BIG BASIN		**CUP** For measuring	
ROLLING-PIN			
CUTTER		**BAKING SHEET** Rub it with a bit of margarine paper to make it greasy	

See that your hands are clean
and your overall on.

Take the big basin and the sieve.
Put the sieve over the basin.
Now put into it
FLOUR . . . . One (1) cup, heaped.
SALT. . . . . One (1) pinch.

Shake the sieve
until all the flour and salt
have fallen into the basin.
Take off the sieve.
Put into the basin
MARGARINE. . . . . . Two (2) small spoons,
. . . . rounded.

Now rub together the flour and fat.
Do it with your finger-tips
until there are no more lumps of fat
left in the flour.
Then wash your hands.
Put in

GRATED CHEESE . . Three (3) big spoons,
. . . . heaped.

Mix in with your finger-tips.
Pour in the
MILK . . . . Four (4) big spoons.
Stir quickly with your blunt knife.
Now you will have to hurry
or your scones will be spoilt.
Sprinkle flour on the table.
Tip out the mixture
and pat it to make it round.
Take your rolling-pin.
Sprinkle it with flour
and roll out the mixture until it is
half ($\frac{1}{2}$) an inch thick.
Take your cutter,
dip it into the flour,
cut out round scones
and place them on the baking sheet.
Gather up the pieces,
Quickly make them into a round
and cut out more scones
until all the bits are used up.
Dip your pastry brush into the milk

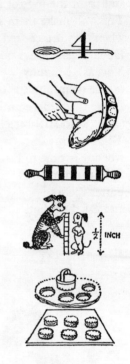

and paint the tops of the scones.
This will make them shiny brown
when they are cooked.
Do all these things quickly.
Now ask Mummy
to put them into the oven.
Leave them there until they are brown,
about 8–10 MINUTES.
Tell Mummy
when it is time to take them out.
Split them in half
butter them
and eat them hot.

~~~~~~

TARTS

Ask Mummy to put the oven on at
Electric 450 or Gas Regulo 8

YOU WILL WANT

MARGARINE

LARD

PLAIN FLOUR

SALT

WATER
In a cup

MILK
In a saucer

BIG BASIN

SIEVE

CUP
for measuring

LARGE SPOON
For measuring

ROLLING-PIN

BLUNT KNIFE

FORK

CUTTER

PASTRY BRUSH

TART TINS
Take a buttery piece
of paper and grease
the tins

Wipe the table with a dry cloth.
Hands washed and overall on?

Take the big basin and into it put
MARGARINE......One (1) big spoon,
...............rounded.
LARD ....One (1) big spoon,
...............rounded.

Squeeze together to make one lump.
Wash your hands.
Now take the sieve
and put it over the big basin.
Into the sieve put
PLAIN FLOUR ....One (1) cup.
SALT...........One (1) pinch.
Shake the sieve
until all the flour and salt
have fallen into the basin.

Now rub together the flour and fat.
Do it with your finger-tips
until there are no more lumps of fat
left in the flour.
Then wash your hands.

Now get your cup of water
and your blunt knife.
Make a hole in the flour
with the knife
and put in
WATER..........Three (3) big spoons.
Mix it into the flour.
If you want more water, put in
a very little and stir well.
Too much water will spoil it.
The mixture should be in one lump
with none left on the inside of the basin.
Take your rolling-pin.
Sprinkle it with flour
and sprinkle flour on to the table.
Tip the pastry out of the basin
on to the table.
Roll it out until it is quite thin.
Take your cutter.
Cut out the pastry
and put it into the tart tins.

Now take your fork
and prick all over the bottom
of each tart.
Press the tip of the fork
round the edge of the tart
to make a pattern.
Next dip your pastry brush
into the milk
and paint over the tarts.
Do not put on too much milk.
The milk will make them shiny brown
when they are cooked.
Then ask Mummy
to put them into the oven for about
12–15 MINUTES.
Tell Mummy
when it is time to take them out.
Now put the tarts into the larder
for 15 minutes, to cool.

WHAT TO PUT INTO YOUR TARTS

JAM or LEMON CURD
Put.............JAM or LEMON CURD
...............One (1) small spoon
into each tart.
Drop thick CREAM on top if you like.
COOKED FRUIT ...APPLES. PEARS.
Put.............APPLES or PEARS
...............One (1) small spoon
into each tart.
Chop up some NUTS
and sprinkle on the top.
COOKED FRUIT ...PLUMS. DAMSONS.
Put.............PLUMS or DAMSONS
...............One (1) on each tart.
Sprinkle CASTER SUGAR on the top.
COOKED FRUIT.BLACKBERRIES. CURRANTS.
Put ..........BLACKBERRIES, CURRANTS
.............One (1) small spoon
on to each tart.
Do not put in any of the juice.
Drop thick CREAM on top if you like.

FRESH FRUIT. RASPBERRIES.
STRAWBERRIES. CURRANTS
LOGANBERRIES OR ANY
OTHER RIPE FRUIT.

Wash all fruit well.

Squash them a little with a spoon.

Sprinkle with CASTER SUGAR.

Put............FRESH FRUIT

...............One (1) small spoon

into each tart.

FRESH FRUIT AND HONEY.

Put............HONEY, stiff kind

...............One (1) small spoon

into each tart.

Then drop in a few currants,

halved raspberries, loganberries,

blackberries or grapes.

FRESH FRUIT.....APPLES AND NUTS

Grate an apple into a basin.

Mummy will show you.

Mix in some CASTER SUGAR and HONEY

Chop up some nuts

and mix them in too.

Put............One (1) small spoon

into each tart.

WHAT TO PUT INTO YOUR TARTS

CHEESE AND TOMATO

YOU WILL WANT

CHEESE

GRATER

TOMATOES
Wash well

KNIFE

PLATE

PEPPER

Take your knife.
Cut the TOMATO into slices.
Put one slice into each tart.
Sprinkle with a little PEPPER.
Now take your grater
and put it over the plate.
Grate the CHEESE into it.
Mummy will show you.

Sprinkle a little cheese
over each slice of tomato.
You can decorate the tarts
with drops of salad cream
and tiny sprigs of parsley.

OTHER FILLINGS

Chopped ham.
Chopped kipper.

Shrimps.
Prawns.
Chopped chicken.
Chopped up egg and bacon.
Put.............One (1) small spoon
into each tart.
Put a drop of salad cream
or mayonnaise
on the top.

What To Put Into Your Tarts

CHEESE AND ONIONS

You Will Want

CHEESE

SPRING ONIONS
Wash well

SALAD CREAM

GRATER

KNIFE

BIG BASIN

SMALL SPOON

Take the big basin.
Put the grater over it.
Take the CHEESE
and grate it into the basin.
Mummy will show you.
Now take the knife
and the SPRING ONIONS.

Cut off the green tops
and chop them up
into small pieces.
Put them into the basin.
Take the SALAD CREAM.
Put in ....One (1) small spoon
into the basin.
Now stir them all together.
Put.............One (1) small spoon
of the mixture
into each tart.

BIG CHERRY CAKE

*Ask Mummy to put the oven on at
Electric 350 or Gas Regulo 4*

You Will Want

FLOUR
Self Raising

SMALL BASIN

SALT

CUP
For measuring

MARGARINE

SIEVE

CASTER SUGAR

CHERRIES
Glacé

WOODEN SPOON
For mixing

EGG

FORK

KNIFE

MILK
In a cup

SALT SPOON

ESSENCE
Vanilla

SMALL CAKE TIN
About 7 inches.
Ask Mummy
to line it

BIG BASIN

Hands washed and overall on?

Take the big basin and the sieve.
Put the sieve over the basin.
Now into the sieve put
FLOUR . . . . Two (2) cups.
SALT . . . . One (1) pinch.

Shake the sieve
until all the flour and salt
have fallen into the basin.
Take off the sieve.
Put into the basin
MARGARINE . . . . . . Four (4) big spoons,
. . . . rounded.

Now rub together the flour and fat.
Do it with your finger-tips
until there are no more lumps of fat
left in the flour.
Then wash your hands.
Count out
CHERRIES . . . . Sixteen (16).

Take your knife
and cut each cherry
into four (4) pieces.
Drop them into the flour.
Rub them around
so that they do not stick together.
Next put in
SUGAR . . . . Five (5) big spoons.
Take your wooden spoon
and mix them all together.
When it is mixed
make a hole in the middle
ready for the egg.
Now take the small basin and the
EGG.
Break the egg into the small basin
and with the fork
beat up the egg.
Then from the cup take
MILK . . . . Five (5) big spoons.
Mix it into the egg.

Add
VANILLA ESSENCE. One (1) salt spoon.
Stir them all together.
Pour into the hole in the big basin,
and with the wooden spoon
mix them gently together.
Spoon the mixture into your cake tin,
smooth the top with your knife
and ask Mummy
to put the cake into the oven.
Leave it there for about
ONE AND A QUARTER (1¼) HOURS.
Tell Mummy
when it is time to take it out.
Let it cool,
then turn it out of the tin.
Ice it and decorate with cherries.

BIG FRUIT CAKE

Ask Mummy to put the oven on at
Electric 350 or Gas Regulo 4

You Will Want

FLOUR
Self Raising

SALT

MARGARINE

CASTER SUGAR

EGG

MILK
In a cup

CURRANTS

SULTANAS

CHOPPED PEEL
If you like it

SMALL BASIN

BIG BASIN

CUP
For measuring

SIEVE

SMALL SPOON

FORK and KNIFE

2 BIG SPOONS
For measuring

WOODEN SPOON
For mixing

CAKE TIN
About 7 inches.
Ask Mummy
to line it

Hands washed and overall on?

Take the big basin
and the sieve.
Put the sieve over the basin.
Now into the sieve put

FLOUR . . . . Two (2) cups.
SALT. . . . . One (1) pinch.
Shake the sieve
until all the flour and salt
have fallen into the basin.
Take off the sieve.
Put into the basin

MARGARINE. . . . . . Four (4) big spoons,
. . . . rounded.
Now rub together the flour and fat.
Do it with your finger-tips
until there are no more lumps of fat
left in the flour.
Then wash your hands.
Next put in

SUGAR . . . . Five (5) big spoons.
CURRANTS. . . . . . . Two (2) big spoons.
SULTANAS . . . . Two (2) big spoons.
If you want it fruity
put in a little more.

CHOPPED PEEL . . . One (1) small spoon.
Mix together with your wooden spoon.
When it is mixed

make a hole in the middle
ready for the egg.
Now take the small basin and the
EGG.
Break the egg into the small basin
and with the fork
beat up the egg.
Then from the cup take
MILK . . . . Five (5) big spoons.
Mix it into the egg
and stir them together.
Pour into the hole in the big basin
and with your wooden spoon
mix them gently together.
Spoon the mixture into your cake tin,
smooth the top with your knife
and ask Mummy
to put the cake into the oven.
Leave it there for about
ONE AND A QUARTER (1¼) HOURS.
Tell Mummy
when it is time to take it out.
Let it cool,
then turn it out of the tin.
If you like you can ice it
and decorate it with nuts.

COCONUT BISCUITS

Ask Mummy to put the oven on at
Electric 350 *or Gas Regulo* 4

You Will Want

PLAIN FLOUR

BAKING POWDER

CASTER SUGAR

BUTTER

DESICCATED
COCONUT

EGG

BIG BASIN

SMALL BASIN

ROLLING-PIN

CUTTER
Fancy or plain

FORK

WOODEN SPOON
For mixing

CUP
For measuring

2 BIG SPOONS

BAKING SHEET
Grease with a bit
of buttery paper

Wash your hands. Overall on.

Take the big basin
and into it put
PLAIN FLOUR .... One (1) cup.
BAKING POWDER . One (1) pinch.
SUGAR .... Two (2) big spoons,
.... heaped.
Take your wooden spoon
and mix them all together.
Next put into the basin
BUTTER .... Two (2) big spoons,
.... rounded.
Now rub together
the flour, fat and sugar.
Do it with your finger-tips
until there are no more lumps of fat
left in the flour.
Then wash your hands.
Next put in
COCONUT........ Three (3) big spoons,
.... heaped.
Now take the small basin and the
EGG.
Break the egg into the small basin
and with the fork
beat up the egg.
Pour into the flour

EGG . . . . Two (2) big spoons.
Mix it all together
until it is in one lump,
firm but not sticky.
If it is too dry
put in some more egg.
Take your rolling-pin.
Sprinkle it with flour
and sprinkle flour on to the table.
Tip out the mixture,
and roll it until it is quite thin.
Take your fork and prick it all over.
Next take your cutter,
dip it into the flour
and cut out the biscuits.
Gather up the bits
and make them into more biscuits.
Put them on to the baking sheet.
Then ask Mummy
to put them into the oven.
Leave them there
until they are golden brown,
about 15–20 MINUTES.
When they are quite cold,
keep them in an airtight tin.

CURRENT BISCUITS

Ask Mummy to put the oven on at
Electric 350 or Gas Regulo 4

You Will Want

PLAIN FLOUR		ROLLING-PIN	
BAKING POWDER		ROUND CUTTER	
SALT		FORK	
CASTER SUGAR		SMALL SPOON	
EGG		2 BIG SPOONS For measuring	
CURRANTS			
GRATED LEMON RIND		WOODEN SPOON For mixing	
BUTTER		CUP	
BIG BASIN		BAKING SHEET Grease with a bit	
SMALL BASIN		of buttery paper	

Wash your hands. Overall on.

Take a big basin
and into it put
PLAIN FLOUR ....One (1) cup.
BAKING POWDER .One (1) pinch.
SALT............One (1) pinch.
Take your wooden spoon
and mix them all together.

Next put into the basin
BUTTER ....Two (2) big spoons,
...............rounded.

Now rub together
the flour and the fat.
Do it with your finger-tips
until there are no more lumps of fat
left in the flour.
Then wash your hands.

Next put in
SUGAR ....Two (2) big spoons.
CURRANTS.......One (1) big spoon.
GRATED
LEMON RIND.....One (1) small spoon.

Take your wooden spoon
and mix them all together.
Now take the small basin and the
EGG.
Break the egg into the small basin
and with the fork
beat up the egg.
Pour into the big basin

EGG .... Six (6) small spoons.
Mix it all together
until it is in one lump,
firm but not sticky.
If it is too dry
put in some more egg.
Take your rolling-pin.

Sprinkle it with flour
and sprinkle flour on to the table.
Tip out the mixture
and roll it until it is quite thin.
Take your fork and prick it all over.

Next take the cutter,
dip it into the flour
and cut out the biscuits.
Gather up the bits
and make them into more biscuits.
Put them on to a baking sheet.
Then ask Mummy
to put them into the oven.
Leave them there
until they are golden brown,
about 15–20 MINUTES.
When they come out of the oven
sprinkle them with sugar.
Leave them to cool.
Keep them in an air-tight tin.

ROLLED OAT BISCUITS

Ask Mummy to put the oven on at
Electric 375 or Gas Regulo 5

YOU WILL WANT

ROLLED OATS

PLAIN FLOUR

CASTER SUGAR

SALT

BAKING POWDER

BUTTER

MILK
In a cup

BIG BASIN

KNIFE

WOODEN SPOON
For mixing

CUTTER

PASTRY BRUSH

CUP
For measuring

BIG SPOON

BAKING SHEET
Grease with a bit
of buttery paper

Wash your hands. Overall on.

Take the big basin
and into it put
ROLLED OATS . . . . One (1) cup.

PLAIN FLOUR . . . . Two (2) big spoons,
. . . . rounded.

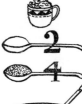

SUGAR . . . . Four (4) big spoons.

SALT. . . . . One (1) pinch.

BAKING POWDER. One (1) big pinch.
Take your wooden spoon
and mix them all together.
Next put into the basin
BUTTER . . . . Two (2) big spoons,
. . . . rounded.

Rub it in.
Do it with your finger-tips
until there are no more lumps of fat
left in the basin.
Then wash your hands.
From the cup take
MILK . . . . One (1) big spoon.

Pour it into the big basin
and mix it all together

until it is in one lump,
firm but not sticky.
If it is too dry
put in some more milk.
Tip the mixture on to the table.
Take your knife
and cut it up into small pieces.
Sprinkle flour on to your hands
and roll the pieces into balls.
Put them on to the baking sheet.
Pat each ball down flat
with your fingers.
Dip your pastry brush into the milk
and paint the top of each biscuit.
Ask Mummy to put them into the oven.
Leave them there
until they are light brown,
about 20 MINUTES.
When they are cool, you can ice them.
Keep them in an air-tight tin.

SANDWICHES

Before you make any sandwiches,
put on your overall and wash your hands.

Sandwiches can be made from

BREAD .... Cut loaves.

PLAIN BISCUITS .. Cream Crackers, Crisp-
breads, Water Biscuits,
etc.

SLIGHTLY SWEET. Digestives or Whole-
meal Biscuits.

ROLLS.

OATCAKES.

Sandwiches can be

OPEN .... With no bread or biscuit
on the top.

CLOSED .... With bread or biscuit on
top as well as under-
neath.

SHAPE

If they are made of bread they can be cut

PLAIN .... In four pieces.

FANCY .... Round, or shaped with a
sandwich or pastry
cutter.

Open Sandwiches

*These can be taken in your hand
or eaten with a knife and fork*

SHRIMP SANDWICHES

You Will Want

SLICED BREAD

SHRIMPS

LETTUCE LEAVES
Well washed

TOMATO SLICES

MAYONNAISE

SALT

PEPPER

KNIFE
For spreading

Butter a slice of bread.
Put a lettuce leaf on it
and cover it
with tomato slices.
Sprinkle with salt and pepper.
Now put on your shrimps
and a few drops
of mayonnaise.

COLD MEAT SANDWICHES

You Will Want

BRIDGE ROLLS *or*
SLICED BREAD

BEETROOT SLICES

SOFT BUTTER

SPRING ONIONS
Chopped

COLD MEAT
Beef, chicken or ham

LETTUCE LEAVES
Well washed

SALT

MUSTARD

PEPPER

KNIFE
For spreading

Open the rolls and lay them flat.
Do not cut them quite in half.
Butter them.
Put on a little mustard
if you are using ham or beef.
Cover the roll with a lettuce leaf.
Lay on slices of cold meat and beetroot.
Sprinkle with salt and pepper
and chopped spring onion.

This can also be put on to bread
toasted on one side only.

CHEESE SPREAD SANDWICHES

You Will Want

CRISP BISCUITS

CHOPPED PARSLEY

SOFT BUTTER

TOMATO

GRATED CHEESE
Ask Mummy
to do this

KNIFE

MAYONNAISE

SMALL BASIN
For mixing

Butter the biscuits.
Take your small mixing basin.
Put into it, the chopped parsley,
the grated cheese
and a little mayonnaise.
Mix them all together.
Spread this on to the biscuit.
Put a slice of tomato on top.

APPLE SANDWICHES

*This must be eaten at once
or the apple will go brown*

YOU WILL WANT

WHOLEMEAL BREAD THICK SLICES		SLICED DATES	
SOFT BUTTER		THICK HONEY	
		CASTER SUGAR	
GRATED APPLE Ask Mummy to do this		SMALL BASIN For mixing	
CHOPPED NUTS		KNIFE	

Butter the bread and spread with honey.
Take your small mixing basin.
Put into it,
grated apple and chopped nuts.
Add a little sugar, not too much.
Mix them all together.
Pile on top of the honey.
Put a few slices of dates on the top.

You can spread cream cheese on the bread
instead of the honey.
If you do, make the apple sweeter.

Closed Sandwiches

CREAM CHEESE SANDWICHES

You Will Want

CREAM CHEESE

CUCUMBER

SPRING ONIONS
Chopped

SLICED BROWN BREAD

SOFT BUTTER

KNIFE
For spreading

Butter two slices of bread.
Spread cream cheese on one slice.
Sprinkle with chopped onion.
Lay on thin slices of cucumber.
Press second slice of bread and butter
on the top.
Make as many more as you need.

This filling can also be put on to
Plain biscuits,
oatcakes or
Digestive biscuits.

HAM SANDWICHES

You Will Want

WHITE BREAD
Sliced

SOFT BUTTER

HAM

MUSTARD
Already mixed

LETTUCE,
MUSTARD AND CRESS
Well washed

SALAD CREAM

KNIFE
For spreading

SMALL BASIN

Butter two slices of bread.
Spread a little mustard on one slice.
Now put on a slice of ham.
Chop up the mustard, cress and lettuce.
Put into a basin with the salad cream
and mix them all together.
Spread this mixture over the ham.
Put on the second slice of bread and butter.
Make as many more sandwiches as you need.

This filling can also be used on
Rolls or plain scones.

SARDINE SANDWICHES

You Will Want

BROWN AND WHITE BREAD Sliced		WATER CRESS Well washed	
SOFT BUTTER		SALT AND PEPPER	
SARDINES		SMALL BASIN	
HARD-BOILED EGG Sliced		KNIFE	
SALAD CREAM	 	FORK For mixing	

Butter one slice of brown bread
and one slice of white.
Put into the small basin
the sardines and salt and pepper.
Mix into a paste with your fork.
Spread some of this on to one slice.
Lay on slices of egg.
Spread salad cream on the second slice
and press this on the first slice of bread.

Eat with watercress and tomatoes.

FRUIT AND HONEY SANDWICHES

You Will Want

SLICED BREAD
Brown or white

SOFT BUTTER

THICK HONEY

KNIFE
For spreading

FRESH FRUIT. You can use, CURRANTS,
RASPBERRIES, LOGANBERRIES,
STRAWBERRIES or GARDEN BLACKBERRIES
Wash the fruit and take off the stalks.
Butter two slices of bread.
Put some thick honey on to one slice.
Sprinkle thickly with fruit.
Put the second slice of bread and butter
on the top.
Press very gently and cut carefully.
If you press too hard
the fruit will come out.

This filling can be used on
Plain scones, halved.

PLAIN FONDANTS

You Will Want

ICING SUGAR		ROLLING-PIN	
LEMON		FINE SIEVE	
		SALT SPOON	
EGG		BIG SPOON	
		SMALL SPOON	
		FORK	
BIG BASIN			
SMALL BASIN		SWEET CUTTERS Fancy or plain	
CUP		PLATE	
BLUNT KNIFE For mixing		GREASEPROOF PAPER	

Wash your hands
and put on your overall.

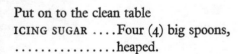

Wipe the table with a dry cloth.

Put on to the clean table
ICING SUGAR ....Four (4) big spoons,
................heaped.

Take the rolling pin.
Roll out all the lumps.
Now take your sieve.
See that it is clean and quite dry.
Put it over your basin
and put in the icing sugar.
Rub it around with your spoon
until it all goes into the basin.
Take the LEMON.
Prick it with a fork.
Squeeze out . . . . . One (1) salt spoon.
Put it into the icing sugar.
Now take the small basin and the
EGG.
Break it gently into the basin.
Put in your spoon.
Carefully take out the yellow yolk.
Put into the cup.
You will not need this.
Now take your fork
and beat up the egg white.
Put into the icing sugar
EGG WHITE . . . . . . Two (2) small spoons.
If you want coloured sweets
ask Mummy to put it in.
COLOURING (whichever you like)
. . . . Two (2) drops
Stir everything together

with your blunt knife
until it is thick and firm
rather like a lump of plasticine.
Sprinkle the table with icing sugar
and tip the mixture out of the basin.
Knead it with your hands
until it is quite smooth.
Keep the table
sprinkled with icing sugar.

Take your rolling-pin
and sprinkle it with icing sugar.

Roll out the mixture
until it is as thick as you want.
Take your cutters
and cut out the sweets.

Gather up the bits
roll them out again
and cut out more sweets.
Do this until
all the bits have been used up.
Put the sweets on to a plate
covered with greaseproof paper,
to dry.

Turn them over, after a while
and then leave until tomorrow.
They should be quite dry.

ORANGE CREAMS

You Will Want

ICING SUGAR

FORK

ORANGE JUICE
In a cup

BLUNT KNIFE

ORANGE RIND
Grated

GREASEPROOF PAPER

LEMON

SWEET CUTTERS
Fancy or plain

ROLLING-PIN

BIG BASIN

BIG SPOON

SIEVE

SALT SPOON

Wash your hands
and put on your overall.

Wipe the table with a dry cloth.

Put on to the clean table
ICING SUGAR.....Three (3) big spoons,
...............heaped.
Take your rolling-pin
and roll out all the lumps.
Now take your sieve.
See that it is clean and quite dry.
Put it over your basin
and put in the icing sugar.
Rub it around with your spoon
until it all goes into the basin.
Now add the grated
ORANGE RIND....One (1) small spoon.
Take the
LEMON.
Prick it with a fork
and squeeze out..One (1) salt spoon.
Put it into the icing sugar.
Now from the cup take
ORANGE JUICE ...Two (2) small spoons.
Put into the icing sugar.
Mix together with your blunt knife
until it is thick and firm
rather like a lump of plasticine.
Sprinkle the table with icing sugar
and tip the mixture out of the basin.
Knead it with your hands
until it is quite smooth.

Keep the table
sprinkled with icing sugar.
Take your rolling-pin
and sprinkle it with icing sugar.
Roll out the mixture
until it is as thick as you want.
Take your cutters
and cut out the sweets.
Gather up the bits,
roll them out again
and cut out more sweets.
Do this
until all the bits
have been used up.
Put some greaseproof paper
on to a plate
and put the sweets on to it.
Leave them until tomorrow to dry.
Turn them over
so that the underneath dries too.
You can decorate them
with hazel nuts or silver balls.

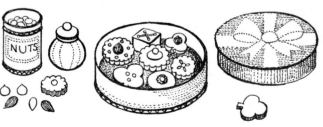

PEPPERMINT CREAMS

You Will Want

ICING SUGAR		SMALL BASIN	
MILK		SMALL SPOON For measuring	
PEPPERMINT ESSENCE		SALT SPOON For measuring	
EGG		GREASEPROOF PAPER	
COLOURING GREEN		2 CUPS	
SWEET CUTTERS Fancy or plain		ROLLING-PIN	
PLATE		FORK	
BIG SPOON		BLUNT KNIFE For mixing	
BIG BASIN		SIEVE	

Wash your hands
and put on your overall.

Wipe the table with a dry cloth.

Put on to the clean table
ICING SUGAR .... Three (3) big spoons
.... heaped.

Take your rolling-pin
and roll out all the lumps.
Now take your sieve.
See that it is clean and quite dry.
Put it over your basin
and put in the icing sugar.
Rub it around with your spoon
until it all goes into the basin.

Now take the small basin and the
EGG.
Break it gently into the basin.
Put in your spoon.
Carefully take out the yellow yolk.
Put it into the cup.
You will not need this.

Now take your fork
and beat up the egg white.
Next take the other cup and put in
MILK . . . . One (1) small spoon.
PEPPERMINT . . . . . One (1) salt spoon.
EGG WHITE . . . . . . One (1) small spoon.
COLOURING. . . . . . Two (2) drops.

Ask Mummy to please do this.
Mix these all together.
Pour into the big basin
with the icing sugar,
and mix together
with your blunt knife
until it is thick and firm
rather like a lump of plasticine.
Sprinkle the table with icing sugar
and tip the mixture out of the basin.
Knead it with your hands
until it is quite smooth.
Keep the table
sprinkled with icing sugar.

Take your rolling-pin
and sprinkle it with icing sugar.
Roll out the mixture
until it is as thick as you want.
Take your cutters
and cut out the sweets.
Gather up the bits
roll them out again
and cut out more sweets.
Do this
until all the bits have been used up.
Put the sweets on to a plate
covered with greaseproof paper,
to dry.
Turn them over, after a while
and then leave until tomorrow.
They should be quite dry.

COFFEE WALNUT CREAMS

You Will Want

ICING SUGAR

COFFEE ESSENCE

EGG

SHELLED WALNUTS

BIG BASIN

SMALL BASIN

CUP

2 SMALL SPOONS
For measuring

BIG SPOON
For measuring

ROLLING-PIN

FORK

BLUNT KNIFE
For mixing

PLATE

GREASEPROOF
PAPER

SIEVE

Wash your hands
and put on your overall.

Wipe the table with a dry cloth.

Put on to the clean table
ICING SUGAR. . . . . Six (6) big spoons,
. . . . .heaped.
Take your rolling pin
and roll out all the lumps.
Now take your sieve.
See that it is clean and quite dry.
Put it over your basin
and put in the icing sugar.
Rub it around with your spoon
until it all goes into the basin.
Now take the small basin and the
EGG.
Break it gently into the basin.
Put in your spoon.
Carefully take out the yellow yolk.
Put it into the cup.
You will not need this.

Now take your fork
and beat up the egg white.
Into the icing sugar put
COFFEE ESSENCE..One (1) small spoon.
EGG WHITE......Two (2) small spoons.

Mix them together
with your blunt knife
until it is thick and firm
rather like a lump of plasticine.
Sprinkle the table with icing sugar
and tip the mixture out of the basin.

Knead it with your hands
until it is quite smooth.
Now, pull off little bits
and roll them into balls
a little bigger than a marble.
Press half a walnut on top of each.

If the walnut will not stick
dip it into the white of egg.
Put some greaseproof paper
on to a plate.
Put the sweets on to the plate
and leave until tomorrow, to dry.

CORN FUDGE

You Will Want

TIN OF SYRUP		EIGHT DATES	
MARGARINE		BIG BASIN	
CASTER SUGAR		CUP For measuring	
SALT		2 BIG SPOONS	
CORNFLAKES		SALT SPOON	
TIN OF DRINKING CHOCOLATE		FLAT *or* SANDWICH TIN	
EIGHT NUTS		KNIFE	
		ROLLING-PIN	

Wash your hands
and put on your overall.

Take the big basin and into it put

SUGAR .... One (1) big spoon.
SALT .... One (1) pinch.
CHOCOLATE ...... Three (3) big spoons.
MARGARINE ...... One (1) big spoon.
If this is hard
ask Mummy to soften it a little.
SYRUP .... One (1) big spoon.
Now take a clean cloth.
On to it put
CORNFLAKES ..... Three (3) cups.
Fold the cloth
and roll it with your rolling-pin.
Now put the crumbs into the basin.
Cut up the
NUTS and DATES
and put them into the basin.

Now take your knife
and mix everything together
very well.
Put a little piece of margarine
on to a bit of paper
and rub it over the tin.
Tip the mixture out of the bowl
into the tin.
Spread it with the knife
and mark it into squares.
Leave it all night to set.
Next day
cut along the lines you have made,
and tip the squares out of the tin.
Keep them in a box.

MARZIPAN DATES

You Will Want

GROUND ALMONDS		BIG SPOON For measuring	
ICING SUGAR		SMALL SPOON	
CASTER SUGAR		CUP	
LEMON		ROLLING-PIN	
VANILLA ESSENCE		BLUNT KNIFE For mixing	
DATES			
EGG		FORK	
BIG BASIN		SALT SPOON	
SMALL BASIN		SWEET CASES	

Wash your hands
and put on your overall.

Take the big basin and into it put
GROUND ALMONDS . Three (3) big spoons.
CASTER SUGAR . . . . . Two (2) small spoons,
. . . . heaped.

Wipe the table with a dry cloth.
Put on to the clean table
ICING SUGAR. . . . . One (1) big spoon,
. . . . heaped.
Take the rolling-pin.
Roll out all the lumps
then spoon it into the big basin.
Now take your blunt knife
and mix everything together.
Now take the small basin and the
EGG.
Break it gently into the basin.
Put in your spoon.
Carefully take out the yellow yolk.
Put it into the cup.
You will not need this.

Now take your fork
and beat up the egg white.
Pour into the big basin
EGG WHITE.....Two (2) small spoons.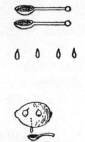
Next ask Mummy to put in
VANILLA ESSENCE...Four (4) drops,
into the egg white.
Then take the
LEMON.
Prick it with a fork
and squeeze out..One (1) salt spoon
and put into the basin.
Mix together with your blunt knife.
If you need it,
pour in a little more egg and stir.
When it is a nice soft lump
tip it on to the table.
Take the stones out of the DATES.
Pull off little pieces of marzipan,
roll into sausages
and press into each date.
Then put into sweet cases, on a plate.

MARZIPAN CHERRIES

Two Ways Of Making Them

Overall on and hands washed.

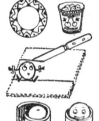

FIRST WAY
Make the marzipan
as you did for the MARZIPAN DATES.
You will want as well
PLATE and GLACÉ CHERRIES.
Roll out the marzipan until it is thin.
Cut it into strips
as wide as a cherry.
Take one of the cherries
and roll a marzipan strip round it.
Let the top of the cherry show.
Put them on to a plate.

SECOND WAY
Make the marzipan the same as before.
Cut up the cherries into little bits
and push them into the marzipan.
Roll it until they are all well mixed.
Roll the marzipan up into little balls.
Put them on a plate to set.

COLOURED MARZIPAN BARS

Overall on and hands washed.
Make the marzipan
as you did for the MARZIPAN DATES.
You will want as well

A SMALL BRUSH   GREEN COLOURING
RED COLOURING   PLATE
       GREASEPROOF PAPER

Tip the lump of marzipan
on to the table.
Cut it up into three pieces.
Put on to the first piece
GREEN COLOURING . . One (1) drop.
Put on to the second piece
RED COLOURING. . . . . One (1) drop.
Leave the third piece, plain white.
Now knead each piece of marzipan
until it looks a nice colour.

Sprinkle some icing sugar
on to the table.
Roll out each piece of marzipan
flat and thin.
Cut into strips
about as wide as a ruler.
Take the red strip
and paint the top with white of egg.
Put the white strip on the top.
Paint this with white of egg.
Put the green strip on the top.
Press them down gently with your hand.
Go on making coloured piles of marzipan
until it is all used up.
Wrap the piles in greaseproof paper,
put them on a plate
and place the plate in the larder
until they are firm.
Take off the greaseproof paper
and cut each pile up into squares.

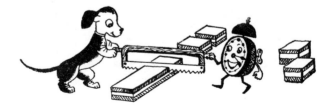

MARZIPAN FRUIT

Overall on and hands washed.
Make the marzipan
as you did for the MARZIPAN DATES.
Divide the marzipan
into little lumps.
Shape these into
APPLES.
PEARS.
STRAWBERRIES.
CHERRIES.
BANANAS.
ORANGES.
LEMONS.
or anything else
that you can think of.

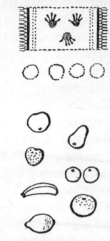

Put the sweets on to a plate.
Leave them there for a day, to set.
Ask Mummy to get her
COOKING COLOURING
and help you to colour the fruit.
Apples..........Red and green.
Pears ....Red, green and yellow.
Strawberries.....Red.
Cherries.........Red.
Oranges.........Orange.
Bananas.........Yellow.
Lemons.........Yellow.
Ask Mummy for some
ANGELICA.
Then if you are clever
cut it up into little pieces
to make the stalks
for your fruit.
Put them on to a plate to dry.

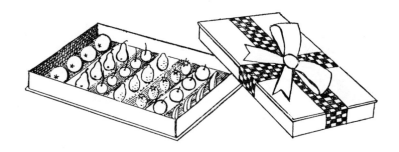

WATER ICING

FOR SMALL CAKES, BUNS OR BISCUITS

You Will Want

ICING SUGAR		ROLLING-PIN	
WARM WATER In a cup		SIEVE	
		KNIFE	
FLAVOURING		SMALL SPOON For measuring	
COLOURING			
SMALL BASIN		PLATE	
BIG SPOON		SALT SPOON	

Wash hands and overall on.
See that the table is clean
and quite dry.

Put on to the table
ICING SUGAR..... Three (3) big spoons,
.... heaped.

Take the rolling-pin.
Roll out all the lumps.
Now take your sieve.
See that it is clean and quite dry.
Put it over the basin
and put in the icing sugar.
Rub it around with your spoon
until it all goes into the basin.

Now put in
WARM WATER.... Three (3) small spoons.
If you want coloured icing
ask Mummy
to put in the COLOURING now.
Mix them all together.

If you want LEMON icing, put in
LEMON..........One (1) salt spoon.
If you want ORANGE icing, put in
ORANGE.........One (1) salt spoon.
If you want VANILLA icing, put in
VANILLA
FLAVOURING.....One (1) salt spoon.
Mix the flavouring in well.
The icing should be a little runny
but not too much
or it will run off.

TO ICE SMALL CAKES, BUNS OR BISCUITS
Stand them on a plate.
Take a spoonful of icing.
Drop it on to whatever you are icing.
Let it run all over.
Allow the icing to set a little.
Put on some more icing if it needs it.
Allow this to set
and then decorate it.

WATER ICING

FOR A BIG CAKE

You Will Want

ICING SUGAR		ROLLING-PIN	
WARM WATER In a cup		SIEVE	
FLAVOURING		KNIFE	
COLOURING		SMALL SPOON	
SMALL BASIN		PLATE	
BIG SPOON		SALT SPOON	

Wash hands and overall on.
See that the table is clean
and quite dry.

Put on to the table
ICING SUGAR..... Six (6) big spoons,
................heaped.
Take the rolling-pin.
Roll out all the lumps.
Now take your sieve.
See that it is clean and quite dry.
Put it over the basin
and put in the icing sugar.
Rub it around with your spoon
until it all goes into the basin.
Now put in
WARM WATER.... Five (5) small spoons.
If you want coloured icing
ask Mummy
to put in the COLOURING now.
Mix them all together.
Now for the FLAVOURING.
If you want LEMON icing, put in
LEMON.......... Two (2) salt spoons.
If you want ORANGE icing, put in

ORANGE.........Two (2) salt spoons.
If you want VANILLA icing, put in
VANILLA
FLAVOURING.....Two (2) salt spoons.

Mix the flavouring in well.
The icing should be a little runny
but not too much
or it will run off.

TO ICE A CAKE
Put it on an upside-down plate.
Put some clean paper
underneath the plate.

Pour the icing
over the top of the cake
and let it run down the sides.
Dip your knife
into the warm water
and smooth the icing down the sides.
Do not touch the top with your knife
or the icing will not shine.

Let it set for a bit.
If you want thicker icing,
put some more on in the same way.
When it is dry
you can decorate it.

DECORATIONS FOR A CAKE

*Here are some of the things
that you can put on the top of a cake*

SILVER BALLS	CHERRIES
SWEETS	CHOCOLATE HAILSTONES
COLOURED SUGAR	CHOCOLATE DROPS
NUTS	CHOCOLATE SHAPES
ANGELICA	SUGAR FLOWERS

HUNDREDS AND THOUSANDS

INDEX